Handwriting Practice Grade 4

Children's Reading & Writing Education Books

PROFESSOR GUSTO
EDUCATIONAL & INFORMATIVE BOOKS FOR CHILDREN
(PRE-K / K-12)

Trace the sentences and rewrite them in the space provided.

I love basketball.

I love basketball.

He loves cooking.

He loves cooking.

Anna loves to eat.

Anna loves to eat.

I have a big dog.

I have a big dog.

I see a blue bird.

I see a blue bird.

This is my kite.

This is my kite.

Richell is playing.

Richell is playing.

Clyde is studying.

Clyde is studying.

Chad is working.

Chad is working.

Bob has a pet cat.

Bob has a pet cat.

We have a plant.

We have a plant.

My dress is red.

My dress is red.

My brother it a lot.

My brother it a lot.

That is a bird.

That is a bird.

This is a pig.

This is a pig.

Look at my toy.

Look at my toy.

The box is green.

The box is green.

This is my pen.

This is my pen.

She can paint.

She can paint.

He can dance.

He can dance.

I can jump.

I can jump.

I like my bike.

I like my bike.

He likes to play.

He likes to play.

She loves to sing.

She loves to sing.

The dog sits.

The dog sits.

My dog can swim.

My dog can swim.

Do you like cake?

Do you like cake?

The bird is here.

The bird is here.

The box is big.

The box is big.

Stop the car!

Stop the car!

My dogs can dig.

My dogs can dig.

Is this a bat?

Is this a bat?

I can read.

I can read.

I can count.

I can count.

The girl is crying.

The girl is crying.

The hat is blue.

The hat is blue.

www.ingramcontent.com/pod-product-compliance
Lightning Source LLC
LaVergne TN
LVHW061323060426

835507LV00019B/2272